BATTLE-READY DINOSAURS

Written by Rosie Rowntree

Illustrated by Marina Halak

First published in 2026 by Hungry Tomato Ltd
F15, Old Bakery Studios, Blewetts Wharf, Malpas Road, Truro, Cornwall,
TR1 1QH, UK.

A CIP catalog record for this book is available from the British Library.

ISBN 9781835696637

Manufactured in the USA

Discover more at
www.hungrytomato.com

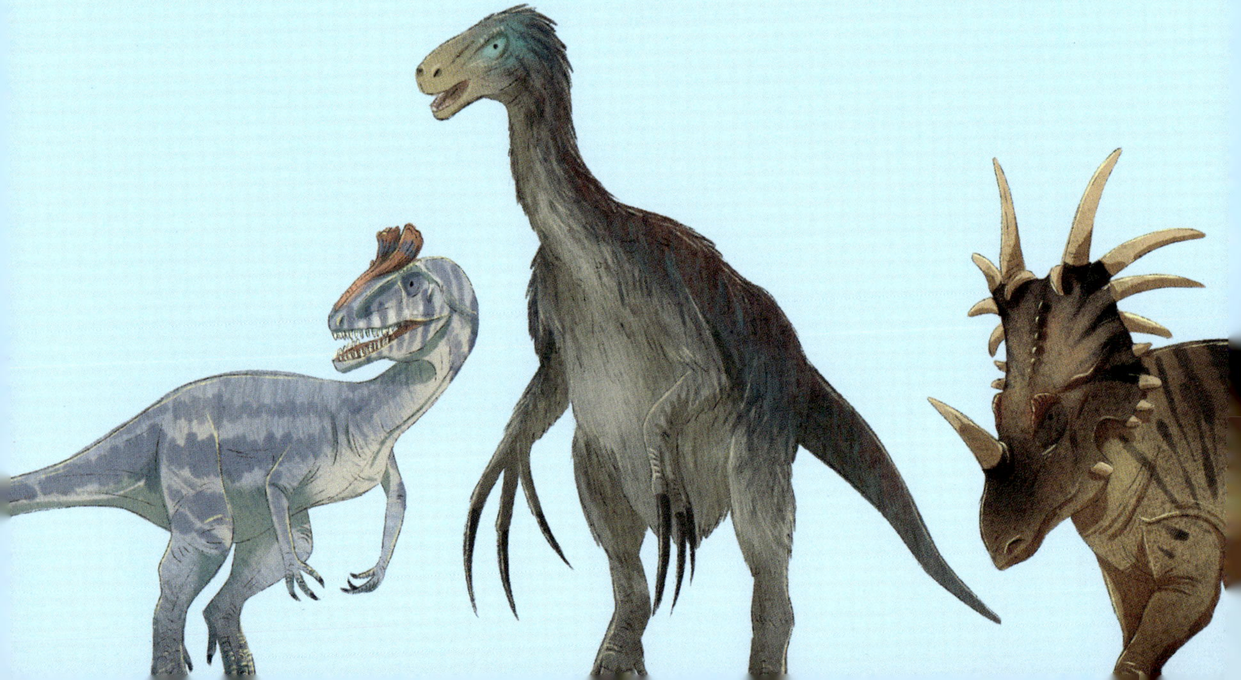

CONTENTS

Words in **BOLD** can be found in the glossary.

THE WORLD OF DINOSAURS

Get ready to explore the wonderful world of dinosaurs! From the iconic Triceratops to the fierce Styracosaurus, there are so many different types of dinosaurs to discover.

WHAT WERE THE DINOSAURS?

Dinosaurs were a group of **reptiles** that lived on Earth millions upon millions of years ago. They ranged in size from the cat-sized Jakapil (page 16) to the truck-sized Amargasaurus (page 23). The word "dinosaur" comes from two Greek words meaning "terrible" and "lizard".

WHEN DID THE DINOSAURS LIVE?

Dinosaurs lived on Earth for almost 180 million years. But they didn't all live at the same time! Some were around later than others. Scientists think that the earliest dinosaurs first appeared over 245 million years ago, while the last roamed the Earth 66 million years ago.

WHAT HAPPENED TO THE DINOSAURS?

66 million years ago, a large **asteroid** hit Earth at incredibly high speed. It caused a lot of fires and sent huge waves crashing across the land. Dust from the asteroid affected the weather and reduced the amount of food that the dinosaurs had to eat.

This made most dinosaurs become **extinct** – except for those that could fly, which survived and developed into the birds that we are familiar with today!

Lambeosaurus (page 20) was one of the last non-bird dinosaurs to walk the Earth.

WHAT ARE FOSSILS?

Fossils are the remains of animals and plants that have been preserved for millions of years. They have been found on all seven of Earth's **continents**! Fossils of a dinosaur's entire **skeleton** are very rare. But even if they are found in bits and pieces, fossils allow scientists to learn a lot about the dinosaurs and their lives!

A Triceratops (page 12) skeleton is one of the most complete dinosaur skeletons ever found!

TYPES OF DINOSAURS

Scientists have arranged the dinosaurs into different categories based on things that they had in common, like their size or the way that they walked.

THEROPODS

Theropods all walked on two legs. Smaller theropods often had feathers, while larger ones were some of the biggest meat-eaters ever!

PACHYCEPHALOSAURS

These dinosaurs also walked on two legs. They are best known, however, for having very tough skulls!

CERATOPSIANS

These plant-eating dinosaurs had large eye-catching frills on their heads that could be used for protection. Their frills also helped them to keep warm in cold weather.

ORNITHOPODS

Ornithopods included several dinosaurs with duck-like beaks and crests on their heads. They were all plant-eaters rather than meat-eaters.

SAUROPODS

Sauropods included some of the largest dinosaurs to ever walk the Earth! They are easy to identify because they all had very long necks and tails, with incredibly small heads in comparison.

STEGOSAURS

Stegosaurs walked on four legs. Their most iconic features are the incredibly tough plates that ran across their backs and provided them with protection.

ANKYLOSAURS

Like stegosaurs, ankylosaurs had protective plates across their bodies. Ankylosaurs, however, had much shorter legs and often had tails that were shaped like clubs.

PTEROSAURS

These reptiles were close cousins of the dinosaurs and were the first animals after insects to develop the ability to fly. The very biggest had a similar wingspan to a small plane!

BATTLE-READY DINOSAURS

Some dinosaurs didn't just survive – they had to fight for their lives! With fearsome features like sharp claws, tough skulls, and powerful tails, these creatures had all the tools they needed to fight off attackers and take down **prey**. Whether striking out alone or finding safety in numbers, the dinosaurs in this book were built for battle!

Weighed as much as an elephant

Therizinosaurus

This huge dinosaur had the longest claws of any animal in history! They were mainly used for hooking onto **vegetation** and pulling it towards its mouth to munch on. But they could also have been used for slashing at any **predator** bold enough to try and take it on.

PRONUNCIATION: THER-ih-zine-oh-SORE-us	**SIZE**
DIET: Herbivore	**SPEED**
TIME PERIOD: Late **Cretaceous**	**DEADLY RATING**

Pachycephalosaurus

Despite being a plant-eater rather than a meat-eater, this dinosaur wasn't afraid of a fight! Pachycephalosaurus had a distinctive dome-shaped head, which it used for ramming into its opponents. Its thick skull helped to protect its brain while it did so.

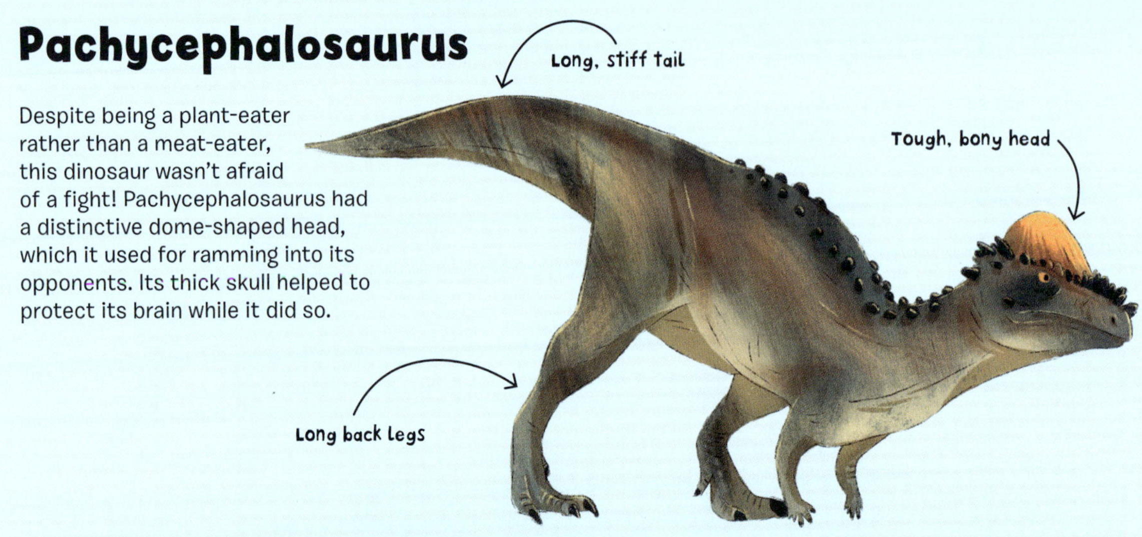

PRONUNCIATION: pack-ee-KEF-al-oh-sore-us

DIET: Herbivore

TIME PERIOD: Late Cretaceous

SIZE

SPEED

DEADLY RATING

Ankylosaurus

Ankylosaurus was the tank of the dinosaur world! Its body was covered in **armor** and spikes, and it had a thick tail like a club. It would have swung this tail like a weapon, fending off predators and fighting for **territory**.

PRONUNCIATION: an-KEE-low-sore-us

DIET: Herbivore

TIME PERIOD: Late Cretaceous

SIZE

SPEED

DEADLY RATING

Achelousaurus

This dinosaur was a cousin of Triceratops (page 12)! It had a distinctive frill on its head which it used to defend itself and to keep its brain cool in warm weather! Two horns at the top of the frill would have been used to fight off other dinosaurs.

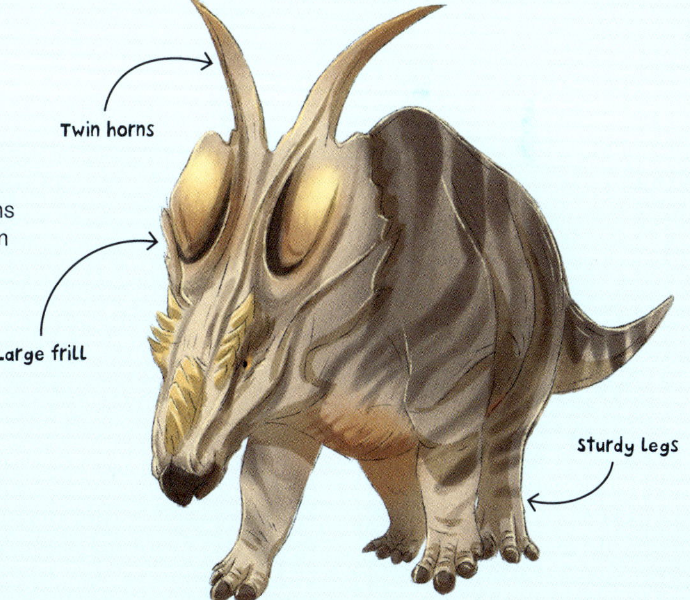

PRONUNCIATION: ah-KEL-oo-SORE-us

DIET: Herbivore

TIME PERIOD: Late Cretaceous

SIZE

SPEED

DEADLY RATING

Triceratops

The intimidating-looking Triceratops had a name that means "three-horned face". Two large horns on its head and a smaller one on its nose – as well as the frill around its neck – made it one of the most easily identifiable dinosaurs of all!

PRONUNCIATION: tri-SER-a-tops

DIET: Herbivore

TIME PERIOD: Late Cretaceous

SIZE

SPEED

DEADLY RATING

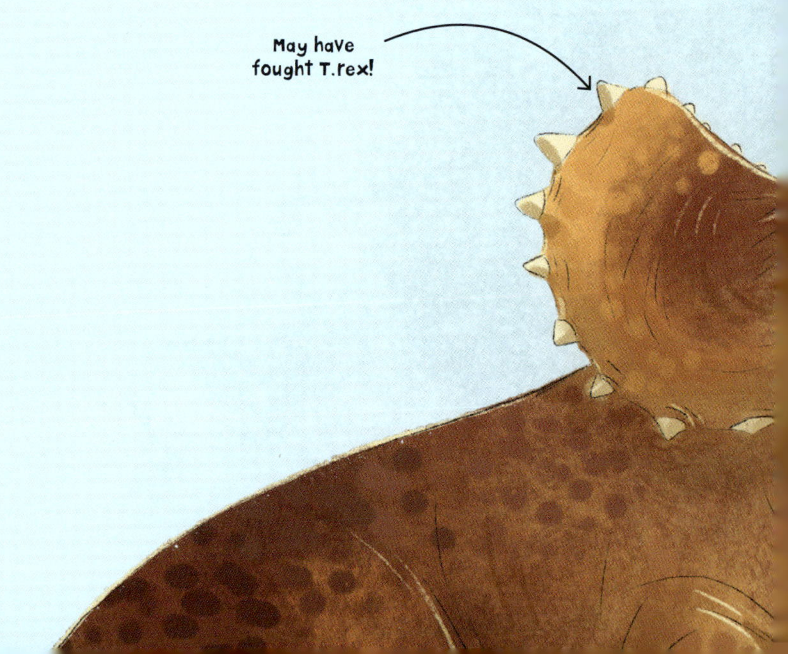

Large horns to help
protect itself
from predators

Euoplocephalus

Heavy and sturdy, Euoplocephalus was well protected by the plating and spikes that covered its back. It even had ridges on its face to help shield its eyelids! Most notable of all was its large club tail that could be swung with immense force to fight off larger dinosaurs.

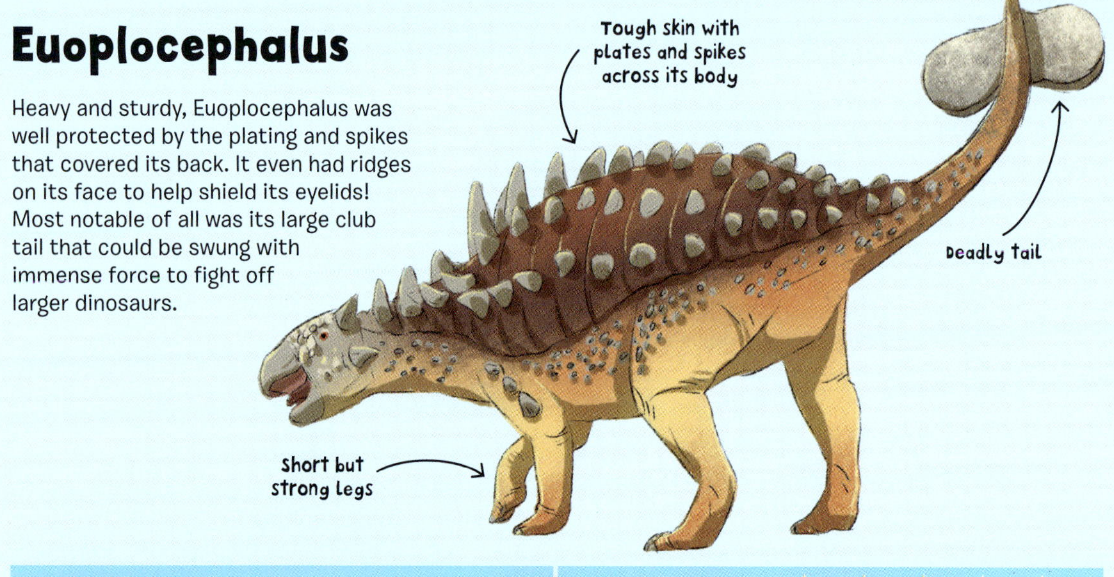

PRONUNCIATION: you-OH-plo-kef-ah-luss

DIET: Herbivore

TIME PERIOD: Late Cretaceous

SIZE

SPEED

DEADLY RATING

Cryolophosaurus

Cryolophosaurus was the first meat-eating dinosaur discovered in what is now Antarctica. It was the largest predator there at the time, and is best identified by the distinctive crest on its head.

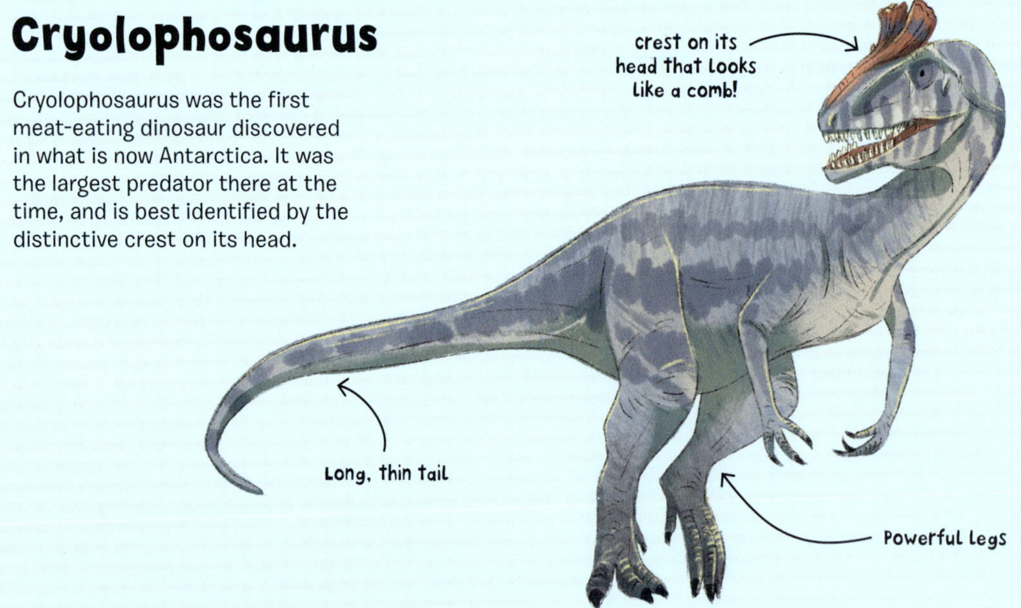

PRONUNCIATION: cry-oh-LOAF-oh-sore-us

DIET: Carnivore

TIME PERIOD: Early **Jurassic**

SIZE

SPEED

DEADLY RATING

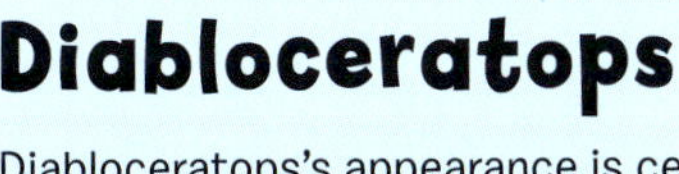

Diabloceratops

Diabloceratops's appearance is certainly impressive! Not only did it have two large horns on its head, it had two even larger, curved ones on top of its frill. One look at it would have been enough to make any dinosaur think twice about attacking!

Intimidating horns

Mouth like a beak

Short, thick tail

PRONUNCIATION: dee-AH-blow-ser-a-tops	SIZE
DIET: Herbivore	SPEED
TIME PERIOD: Late Cretaceous	DEADLY RATING

Stygimoloch

This dinosaur's thick skull and long horns, combined with its speed and agility, made it a tough opponent. That's despite its relatively small size! Some scientists, however, believe that it is actually a young Pachycephalosaurus (page 10) rather than a **species** of its own!

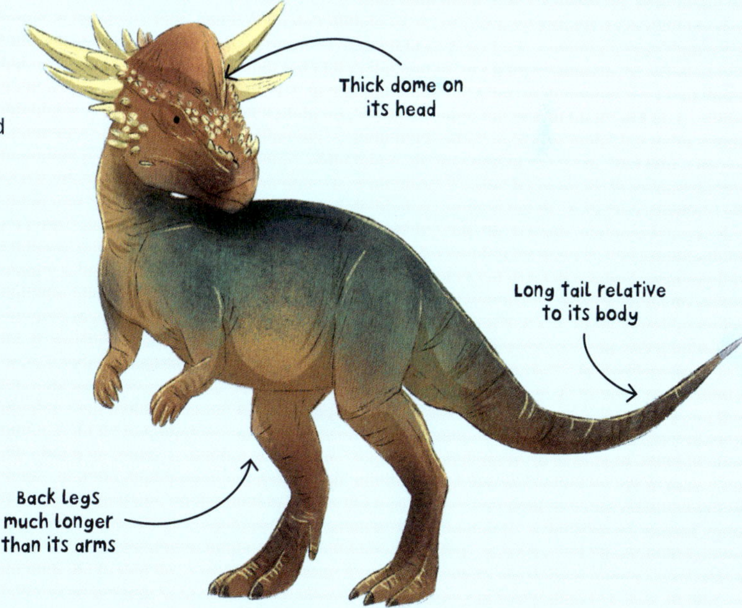

PRONUNCIATION: STIJ-ee-mol-ok	SIZE 
DIET: Herbivore	SPEED
TIME PERIOD: Late Cretaceous	DEADLY RATING

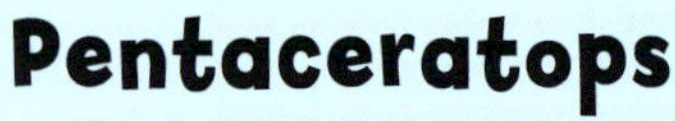

Pentaceratops

Pentaceratops belonged to the same family of dinosaurs as Triceratops (page 12) and has a name that means "five-horned face". It did indeed have five horns: one on its nose, two on top of its head, and two on the side of its head.

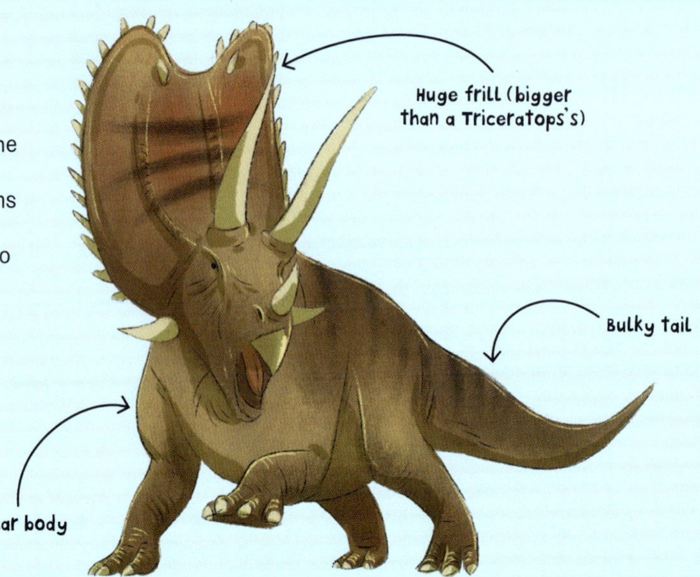

PRONUNCIATION: penta-ah-KER-ah-tops

DIET: Herbivore

TIME PERIOD: Late Cretaceous

SIZE

SPEED

DEADLY RATING

Jakapil

The tiny Jakapil is thought to have been no bigger than a cat! But despite its incredibly small size, it wasn't helpless. Jakapil was covered in tough skin from its neck to its tail and had multiple spikes that helped to protect it.

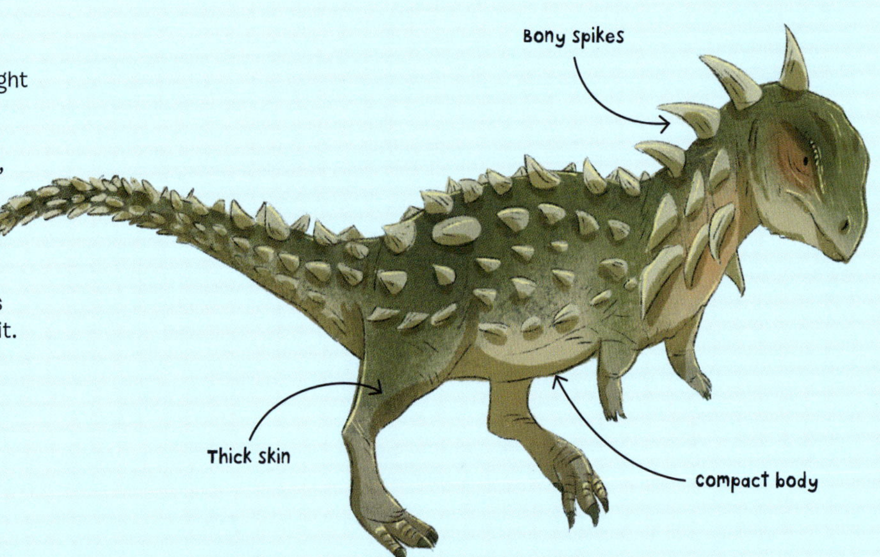

PRONUNCIATION: jah-KAH-pil

DIET: Herbivore

TIME PERIOD: Late Cretaceous

SIZE

SPEED

DEADLY RATING

Stegoceras

Stegoceras was part of the same group of dinosaurs as Pachycephalosaurus (page 10) and shared a similar dome-shaped head. Stegoceras was the smallest member of this group and had a very good sense of smell.

PRONUNCIATION: ste-GO-ser-as

DIET: Herbivore

TIME PERIOD: Late Cretaceous

SIZE

SPEED

DEADLY RATING

Chasmosaurus

Chasmosaurus had smaller horns than other similar dinosaurs but had an incredibly large frill that was the shape of a rectangle. It would have been used to protect Chasmosaurus's neck or to attract a **mate**.

Rectangular frill

Relatively small horns

Mouth like a beak

PRONUNCIATION: KAZ-mo-sore-us

DIET: Herbivore

TIME PERIOD: Late Cretaceous

SIZE

SPEED

DEADLY RATING

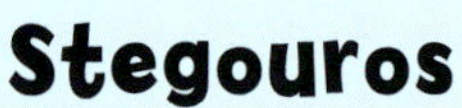

Stegouros

Stegouros was related to dinosaurs like Ankylosaurus (page 11) but had a slightly different tail. Stegouros's was wide and flat rather than rounded, and would have been waved from side to side to scare predators.

Tough bones sticking out for protection

Short, flat club tail

Stocky body

PRONUNCIATION: ste-GOR-os

DIET: Herbivore

TIME PERIOD: Late Cretaceous

SIZE

SPEED

DEADLY RATING

Kosmoceratops

While Lokiceratops (page 19) had the longest frill horns of any horned dinosaur, Kosmoceratops had the most! This made it one of the most impressive dinosaurs to look at!

PRONUNCIATION: COS-mo-SER-ah-tops

DIET: Herbivore

TIME PERIOD: Late Cretaceous

SIZE

SPEED

DEADLY RATING

Lokiceratops

Lokiceratops looked similar to a modern-day rhinoceros! It had the largest frill horns of any horned dinosaur ever, but would have used these for attracting mates or to intimidate other dinosaurs of the same species rather than for fighting.

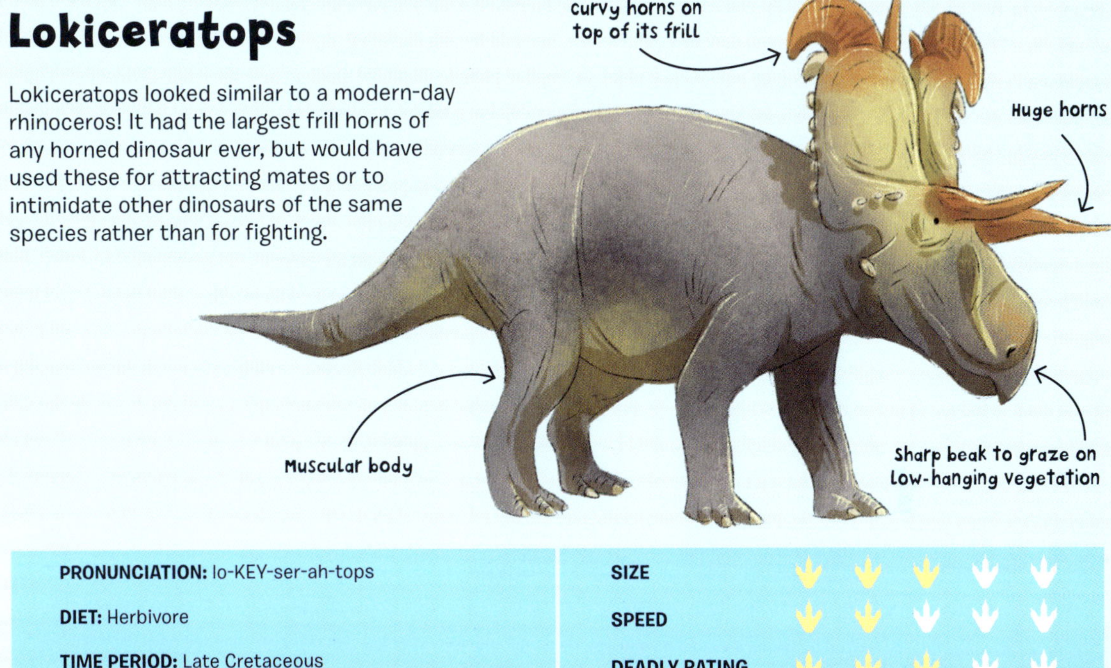

PRONUNCIATION: lo-KEY-ser-ah-tops

DIET: Herbivore

TIME PERIOD: Late Cretaceous

SIZE

SPEED

DEADLY RATING

Huayangosaurus

Like other Stegosaurs, Huayangosaurus had two rows of rigid, spiky plates sticking up from its back. It also had several spikes near the end of its tail to use if any larger predator got too close.

PRONUNCIATION: hoy-YANG-oh-SORE-us

DIET: Herbivore

TIME PERIOD: Mid Jurassic

SIZE

SPEED

DEADLY RATING

Lambeosaurus

Lambeosaurus was a type of “duck-billed” dinosaur, a group of dinosaurs that got their names because of their flattened snouts. Despite the shape of its snout, Lambeosaurus still had a lot of teeth, which it could quickly and easily replace if any got worn down while chewing on plants.

PRONUNCIATION: lam-BEE-oh-SORE-us

DIET: Herbivore

TIME PERIOD: Late Cretaceous

SIZE

SPEED

DEADLY RATING

Styracosaurus

The defining feature of Styracosaurus was its impressive nose horn that looked like a rhino’s. It was a heavy dinosaur and likely not very fast. Because it couldn’t run away from large predators, it instead found safety in numbers and lived in herds to protect itself.

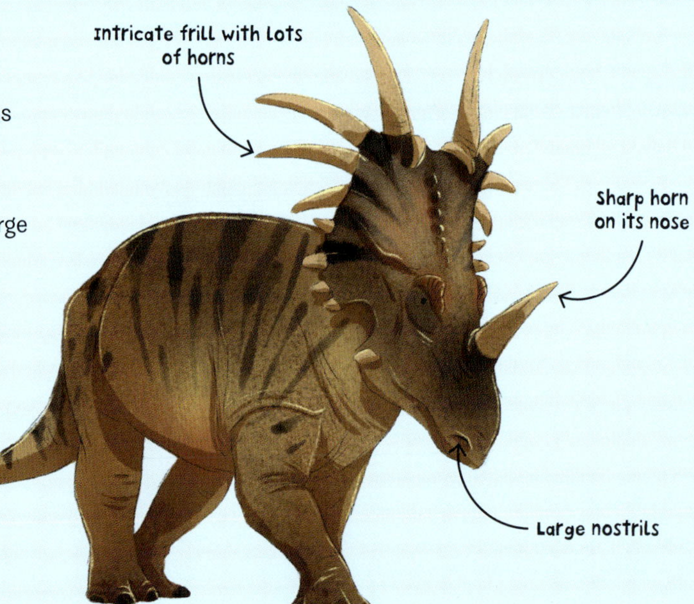

PRONUNCIATION: sty-RAK-oh-sore-us

DIET: Herbivore

TIME PERIOD: Late Cretaceous

SIZE

SPEED

DEADLY RATING

Gastonia

This well-protected dinosaur had two especially large spikes over its shoulders. It lacked the club tail of its relatives but it still had the tough appearance to avoid attacks from other dinosaurs.

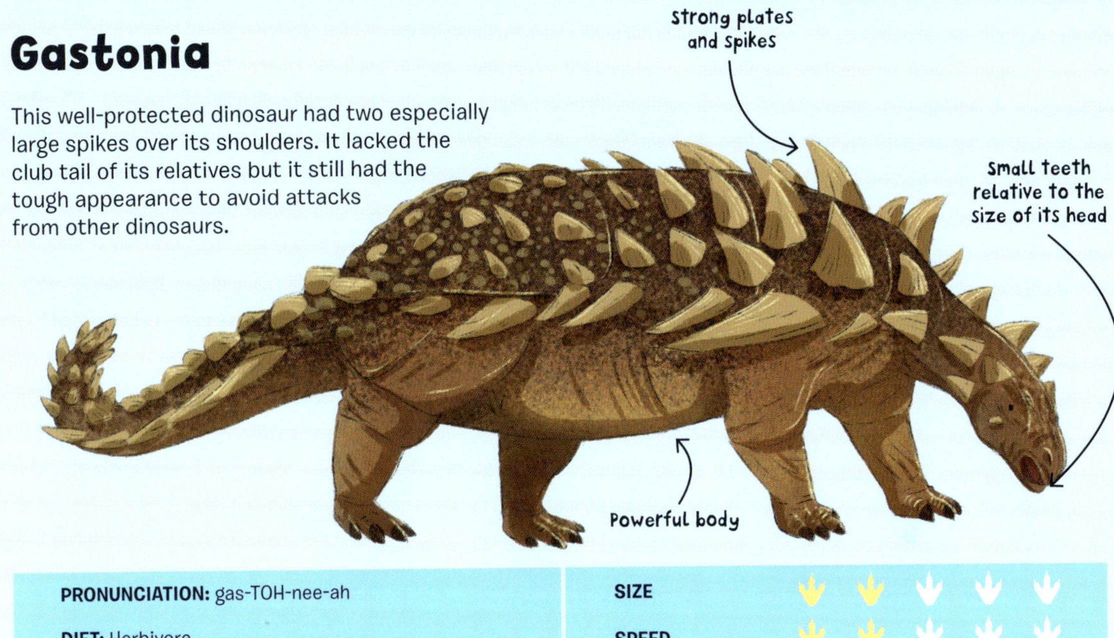

PRONUNCIATION: gas-TOH-nee-ah

DIET: Herbivore

TIME PERIOD: Early Cretaceous

SIZE

SPEED

DEADLY RATING

Ouranosaurus

Ouranosaurus is another duck-billed dinosaur like Lambeosaurus (page 20). It had rows of tightly-packed teeth ideal for chomping on vegetation and could rear up on its back legs to reach any food higher up.

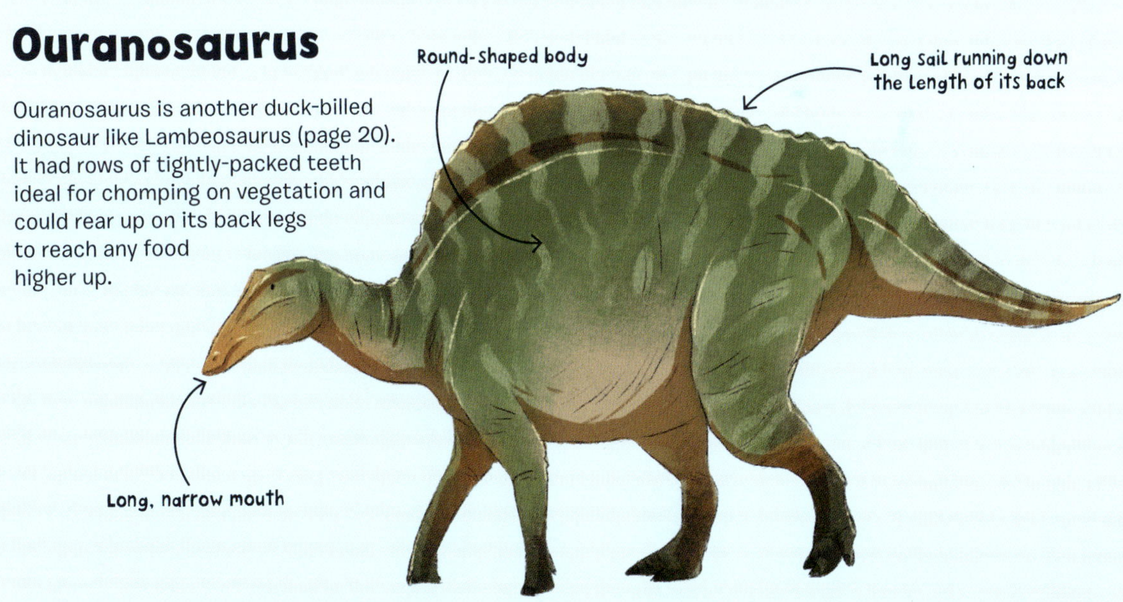

PRONUNCIATION: oo-RAH-noh-sore-us

DIET: Herbivore

TIME PERIOD: Early Cretaceous

SIZE

SPEED

DEADLY RATING

Nodosaurus

Unlike most of its relatives, Nodosaurus didn't have protective spikes on its head or a tail like a club. It did, however, have the usual tough protective plates across its body. Because of its short neck, it would have only eaten from vegetation close to the floor.

PRONUNCIATION: no-doh-SORE-us

DIET: Herbivore

TIME PERIOD: Early Cretaceous

	Rating (out of 5)
SIZE	3
SPEED	2
DEADLY RATING	2

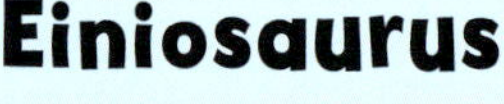

Einiosaurus

Einiosaurus shared many traits with other Ceratopsian dinosaurs, including a large frill with horns on top, and a muscular body. However, the horn on Einiosaurus's nose curved downward rather than up. This would have made it difficult to use in a fight against a predator.

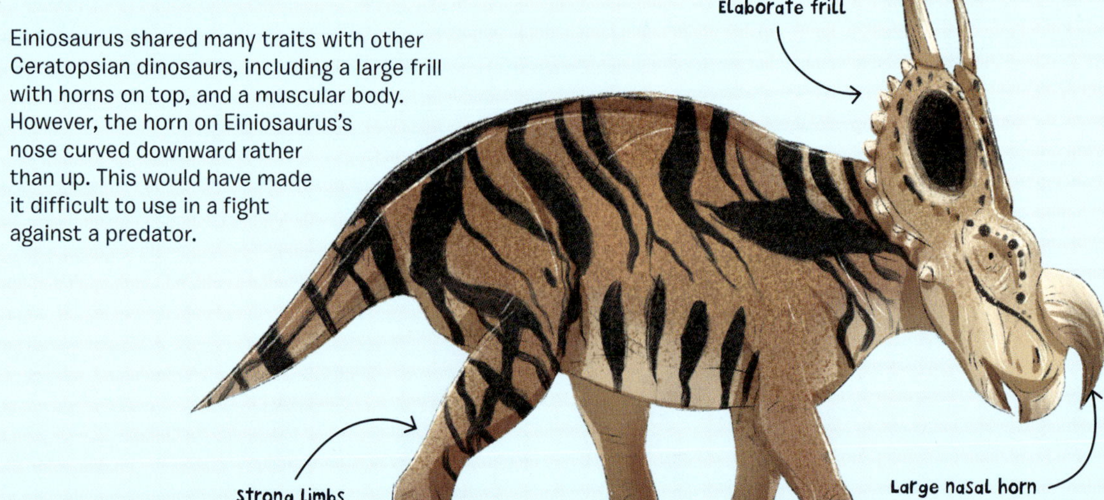

PRONUNCIATION: EE-nee-oh-sore-us

DIET: Herbivore

TIME PERIOD: Late Cretaceous

	Rating (out of 5)
SIZE	3
SPEED	2
DEADLY RATING	3

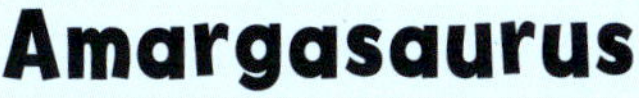

Amargasaurus

The double row of spines along its neck and body gave Amargasaurus a distinctive appearance! What they looked like exactly is still a mystery to science. They could have been individual spikes or horns, or connected by skin like a **sail**.

Tail like a whip!

Double row of spines

Thick neck

PRONUNCIATION: A-MARG-oh-sore-us

DIET: Herbivore

TIME PERIOD: Early Cretaceous

SIZE

SPEED

DEADLY RATING

Eotrachodon

Eotrachodon went about its life on a mixture of two and four legs. Scientists think it walked around mainly on its strong back legs, but came down onto all fours to eat.

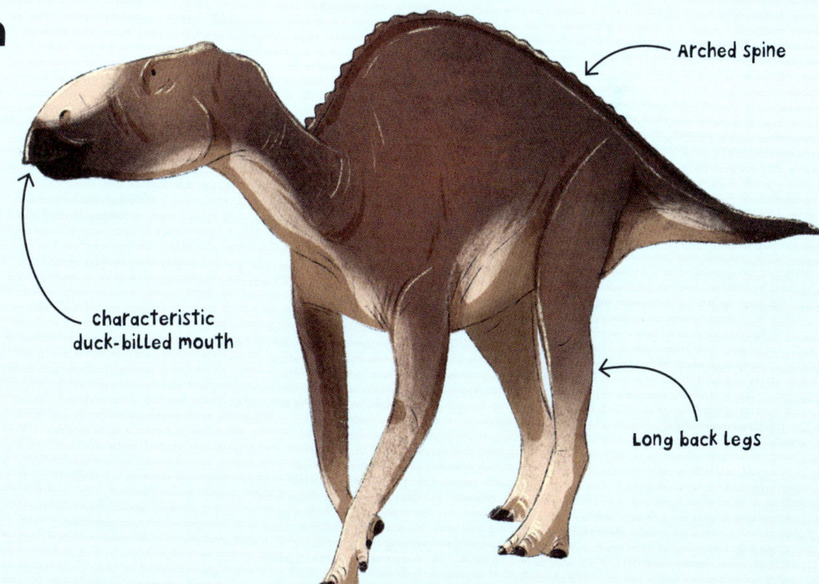

PRONUNCIATION: ee-OH-trak-oh-don

DIET: Herbivore

TIME PERIOD: Late Cretaceous

SIZE

SPEED

DEADLY RATING

DID YOU KNOW?

What more is there to know about these battle-ready dinos? Let's take a look at some amazing facts and find out!

Multiple Triceratops fossils have been discovered with bite marks from T. Rex that later healed, meaning they survived its attacks.

Stegoceras may have been fought by young tyrannosaurs as hunting practice.

Ankylosaurus also had bony plates in its eyelids to protect its eyes.

Some scientists believe that for the Cryolophosaurus to survive in Antarctica, they might have had feathers.

Pachycephalosaurus' skulls were made up of three layers of bone, and the top could be over 10 inches (25 cm) thick.

Pentaceratops' large frills had large openings, meaning they were more for display than for defending themselves in fights.

NAME THAT DINO

Can you name the dinosaur in the picture? Clues have been provided for you based on facts in the book.

CLUE: These dinos were smaller than cats but covered in spikes.

CLUE: These dinos were the first meat-eating dinosaur discovered in what is now Antarctica.

CLUE: These dinosaurs had three horns on their heads, and may have used them to fight T.rex.

CLUE: These dinos had dome-shaped heads, used for ramming into its opponents.

CLUE: These dinos had a double row of spines along their thick necks.

CLUE: These dinos were a type of "duck-billed" dinosaur with large crests on their heads.

CLUE: These dinos had incredibly large, rectangular frills.

CLUE: These dinos were related to Ankylosaurus but had shorter, flatter tails.

CLUE: These dinos were covered in armor and spikes, and used their thick tails as a weapon.

CLUE: These huge dinos had the longest claws of any animal in history.

Answers can be found on page 32.

WHERE DID DINOSAURS LIVE?

Dinosaurs lived all over the world – and in all kinds of places! Let's explore the different environments they called home.

Forests

Some dinosaurs lived in lush, leafy forests filled with tall trees and ferns. These forests were warm and wet, with plenty of plants to eat. Living among the trees helped some dinosaurs hide from predators... or sneak up on their prey!

Plains

Wide, flat land with open space was perfect for dinosaurs that liked to move in big herds. Dinosaurs like Triceratops and Edmontosaurs lived on these open plains, where they could find lots of low plants and keep an eye out for danger.

Deserts

Some dinosaurs lived in dry, sandy places too! These deserts didn't have much water, but clever dinosaurs like Velociraptors could survive by staying cool in the shade and hunting for food. **Fossils** have even been found in desert sand!

Swamps and Wetlands

Swampy areas were wet, muddy, and full of life. Big plant-eaters like Ouranosaurus may have loved these spots, where they could cool off and find soft water plants to eat. Wetlands also had fish, insects, and other tasty treats for smaller dinos.

Volcanic Areas

Some dinosaurs lived near volcanoes! These places were rocky and full of lava streams, but they had rich soil for growing plants after eruptions. Dinosaurs like the Iguanodon may have walked through these landscapes long ago.

GLOSSARY

Armor – a protective outer layer.

Asteroid – a small, rocky object that orbits the Sun.

Carnivore – an animal that only eats meat.

Continents – the huge pieces of land on Earth. For example, Africa and North America are separate continents.

Cretaceous – a period of time that lasted from about 143 to 66 million years ago.

Extinct – a species (see right) of animals with no living members.

Fossils – the remains or impression of plants and animals that lived long ago.

Herbivore – an animal that only eats plants.

Jurassic – a period of time that lasted from about 201 to 143 million years ago.

Mate – two animals that come together to produce young.

Predator – an animal that hunts and kills other animals for food.

Prey – an animal that is hunted by other animals for food.

Reptiles – a group of cold-blooded animals, including snakes, lizards, crocodiles, and some types of dinosaurs.

Sail – a large, flat structure that grows on the backs of certain animals, including some dinosaurs.

Skeleton – the bony frame that supports and protects the body of a person or animal.

Species – a group of living things that share characteristics and features, and can produce young with each other. For example, Stegosaurus and Triceratops are different dinosaur species.

Territory – an area of land that an animal will protect from other animals.

Vegetation - plant life in a particular area.

INDEX

NAME THAT DINO ANSWERS

1 - Jakapil
2 - Cryolophosaurus
3 - Triceratops
4 - Pachycephalosaurus
5 - Amargasaurus
6 - Lambeosaurus
7 - Chasmosaurus
8 - Stegouros
9 - Ankylosaurus
10 - Therizinosaurus

ABOUT THE AUTHOR

Rosie Rowntree is a children's author living in the west of Cornwall. Sharing her love of learning through her writing, she is passionate about sparking curiosity in children as they begin to broaden their horizons and learn about their surroundings - and beyond!

ABOUT THE ILLUSTRATOR

Marina Halak is a talented illustrator of children's books from Ukraine. Her stunning illustrations are inspired by her own childhood, children, nature, magical moments and fairy tales. Marina is also the illustrator behind the related series, *Dogs* and *Cats*.

Picture Credits:
(abbreviations: t=top, b=bottom, m=middle, l=left, r=right)

Shutterstock:
3dMediSphere 24mr (t. rex); Bee_acg 29br (iguanodon); Denis---S 24tl; Herschel Hoffmeyer 28tl, 29ml; Jan Zwolinski 24bl; Limbitech 29br (scenery); Michael Rosskothen 24mr, 25bl; Mr. Aekalak Chiamcharoen 24tm; Oleksandr Matsibura 25tl; Orla 28br; Pavel Chagochkin 29mr; Shvoeva Elena 25mr; Warpaint 29tr.

Every effort has been made to trace the copyright holders, and we apologize in advance for any unintentional omissions. We would be pleased to insert the appropriate acknowledgments in any subsequent edition of this publication.